Contents

Advanced CBT Techniques 50

Applying CBT to Specific Issues 61

CBT and Relationships.....................75

CBT and Self-Care........................86

INTRODUCTION TO CBT

What is CBT?

What is CBT?

Cognitive Behavioral Therapy (CBT) is a type of psychotherapy that focuses on the ways in which our thoughts, feelings, and behaviors are interconnected. The goal of CBT is to help individuals identify and change negative patterns of thinking and behavior that may be contributing to their emotional distress.

CBT is based on the idea that our thoughts, feelings, and behaviors are all interconnected and that changing one can have a positive impact on the others. For example, if we have negative thoughts about ourselves, this can lead to feelings of sadness or anxiety, which can then lead to behaviors such as avoidance or isolation.

CBT is a structured therapy that typically involves a set number of sessions, usually ranging from 8-20. The therapist and client work together to identify specific goals for therapy and develop a plan to achieve those goals. The therapist may use a variety of techniques, such as cognitive restructuring or behavioral activation, to help the client achieve their goals.

One of the key principles of CBT is that it is a collaborative process. The therapist and client work together as a team to identify and challenge negative thoughts and behaviors. The therapist may provide guidance and support, but ultimately it is up to the client to make changes in their own thinking and behavior.

CBT has been shown to be effective in treating a wide range of mental health conditions, including anxiety disorders, depression, and post-traumatic stress disorder (PTSD). It has also been used to treat physical health conditions such as chronic pain and insomnia.

In summary, CBT is a type of psychotherapy that focuses on changing negative patterns of thinking and behavior. It is a collaborative process between the therapist and client and has been shown to be effective in treating a wide range of mental health conditions.

The history of CBT

The history of CBT

Cognitive-behavioral therapy (CBT) is a psychological treatment approach that has gained immense popularity over the past few decades. It is a form of psychotherapy that aims at helping individuals identify and change negative or unhelpful patterns of thinking, feeling, and behavior. CBT has become one of the most widely used and researched forms of psychotherapy, and its success rate is impressive. In this chapter, we will explore the history of CBT and how it has evolved over the years.

The roots of CBT can be traced back to the 1950s and 1960s when behavior therapy emerged as a new approach in psychology. Behavior therapy focused on observable, measurable behaviors, and aimed at changing them using techniques such as reinforcement, punishment, and modeling. However, behavior therapy had its limitations, particularly in treating emotional and cognitive problems. This led to the development of cognitive therapy, which emphasized the role of thoughts and beliefs in shaping behavior and emotions.

In the 1970s, Aaron Beck, a cognitive therapist, developed a comprehensive cognitive model for depression. He proposed that negative automatic thoughts and underlying core beliefs contribute to the development and maintenance of depression. Beck's cognitive model of depression provided a framework for developing cognitive therapy, which aimed at identifying and challenging negative thoughts and beliefs in individuals with depression.

In the 1980s, Albert Ellis, a psychologist, developed Rational Emotive Behavior Therapy (REBT), which was another form of cognitive therapy. REBT focused on identifying and changing irrational beliefs that lead to emotional disturbance. Ellis believed that individuals' emotional reactions are not caused by external events, but rather by the way they interpret or evaluate these events.

Over the years, CBT has continued to evolve and has been applied to a wide range of psychological problems, including anxiety disorders, eating disorders, and personality disorders. The success of CBT has been attributed to its evidence-based approach, which draws on scientific research to develop and evaluate treatment interventions.

In conclusion, the history of CBT is a testament to the power of scientific research and innovation in the field of psychology. CBT has come a long way since its inception and has proven to be an effective and reliable form of psychotherapy. Today, CBT remains an important tool for helping individuals overcome psychological problems and lead happier, more fulfilling lives.

The benefits of CBT

The Benefits of CBT

Cognitive-behavioral therapy (CBT) is a highly effective form of therapy that can help individuals overcome a range of mental health issues. It is a practical and evidence-based approach that has been found to be effective in treating depression, anxiety, post-traumatic stress disorder (PTSD), eating disorders, and many other mental health conditions.

One of the primary benefits of CBT is that it is a short-term and goal-oriented therapy. Compared to traditional therapy, CBT is usually delivered in a shorter period of time and focuses on specific problems or symptoms. This means that individuals can see improvements in their mental health much quicker than they would with other forms of therapy.

Another benefit of CBT is that it is a collaborative and supportive therapy. The therapist and the individual work together to identify negative thinking patterns and behaviors that contribute to their mental health issues. The therapist then helps the individual develop coping skills and strategies to overcome these negative patterns and behaviors.

CBT also teaches individuals skills that they can use for the rest of their lives. Rather than relying on medication or therapy for ongoing support, individuals who receive CBT learn skills that they can use to manage their mental health on their own. This can lead to a greater sense of control and empowerment.

In addition, CBT has been found to be effective in preventing the recurrence of mental health issues. By learning skills to manage negative thinking patterns and behaviors, individuals are better equipped to cope with challenging situations in the future.

Overall, CBT is a highly effective form of therapy that can help individuals overcome a range of mental health issues. It is a short-term and goal-oriented therapy that is collaborative, supportive, and teaches individuals skills they can use for the rest of their lives.

How CBT works

CBT, or Cognitive Behavioral Therapy, is a type of psychotherapy that has been found to be effective in treating a wide range of mental health conditions, including anxiety, depression, and PTSD. In this subchapter, we will explore the basics of how CBT works, and how it can help individuals achieve greater well-being and mental health.

At its core, CBT is based on the principle that our thoughts, feelings, and behaviors are interconnected, and that by changing our thoughts and behaviors, we can change how we feel. CBT is a structured, goal-oriented approach to therapy that involves identifying and challenging negative or unhelpful thoughts and beliefs, and replacing them with more realistic and positive ones.

There are several key components of CBT that make it an effective approach to therapy. One of these is the emphasis on collaboration between the therapist and the client. In CBT, the therapist works with the client to identify their goals for therapy, and to develop a treatment plan that is tailored to their unique needs and circumstances.

Another important aspect of CBT is the use of specific techniques and strategies to help clients challenge and modify their negative thoughts and beliefs. These may include cognitive restructuring, which involves identifying and challenging automatic negative thoughts, or behavioral activation, which involves setting and working towards specific goals to improve mood and wellbeing.

In addition to these core components, CBT also emphasizes the importance of homework and practice outside of therapy sessions. Clients are often given specific assignments or exercises to complete between sessions, in order to reinforce the skills and strategies learned in therapy.

Overall, CBT is a highly effective approach to therapy that is grounded in scientific research and has been shown to be effective in treating a wide range of mental health conditions. By working collaboratively with a trained CBT therapist, individuals can learn to challenge and modify their negative thoughts and beliefs, and develop more positive and realistic ways of thinking and behaving.

THE BASICS OF CBT

The ABCs of CBT

The ABCs of CBT

Cognitive Behavioural Therapy (CBT) is a powerful tool that can help us to understand and manage our thoughts, feelings, and behaviours. The goal of CBT is to identify and change negative patterns of thinking and behaviour that may be holding us back or causing us distress.

CBT is based on the idea that our thoughts, feelings, and behaviours are all interconnected. Our thoughts influence our feelings, which in turn influence our behaviours. By understanding and changing our thoughts, we can change how we feel and behave.

The ABC model is a key concept in CBT. It stands for:

A   –   Activating   event
B   –   Beliefs
C – Consequences

The activating event is the trigger that sets off a chain reaction of thoughts, feelings, and behaviours. It could be anything from a stressful situation at work to a disagreement with a friend.

Our beliefs about the activating event determine how we interpret it and how we respond. If we have negative beliefs, this can lead to negative thoughts, feelings, and behaviours. For example, if we believe that we are not good enough, we may interpret a mistake at work as evidence of our incompetence.

The consequences of our beliefs and behaviours can be positive or negative. If we have positive beliefs and behaviours, we are more likely to have positive outcomes. If we have negative beliefs and behaviours, we are more likely to have negative outcomes.

CBT helps us to identify and challenge negative beliefs and behaviours, and replace them with more positive ones. This can help us to improve our mood, reduce our anxiety, and achieve our goals.

In summary, the ABC model is a simple but powerful tool that can help us to understand how our thoughts, feelings, and behaviours are interconnected. By identifying and changing negative patterns, we can improve our mental health and wellbeing.

Negative thinking patterns

Negative thinking patterns are often the cause of anxiety, depression, and other mental health issues. These patterns can be deeply ingrained and difficult to break, but with the help of cognitive-behavioral therapy (CBT), you can learn how to recognize and challenge them.

One common negative thinking pattern is catastrophizing, where you imagine the worst possible outcome in situations. For example, if you're running late for a meeting, you might think that you'll get fired or lose your job. This type of thinking can lead to excessive worry and anxiety, and it's important to learn how to challenge these thoughts by asking yourself if they're realistic or if there are other, more likely outcomes.

Another negative thinking pattern is jumping to conclusions, where you assume the worst without any evidence. For example, if a friend doesn't respond to your text message, you might assume that they're angry with you or don't want to be friends anymore. It's important to learn how to challenge these assumptions by considering alternative explanations and asking for clarification if necessary.

A third negative thinking pattern is black-and-white thinking, where you see things as either all good or all bad, with no middle ground. For example, if you make a mistake at work, you might think that you're a complete failure and that you'll never be successful. It's important to learn how to challenge this type of thinking by recognizing that things are rarely all good or all bad, and that mistakes are a natural part of learning and growth.

Other common negative thinking patterns include personalization (where you blame yourself for everything), overgeneralization (where you assume that one negative event means everything is bad), and emotional reasoning (where you assume that your feelings are always accurate).

By learning to recognize and challenge these negative thinking patterns, you can improve your mental health and overall well-being. CBT is a powerful tool for overcoming negative thinking, and this book will provide you with a comprehensive course in this approach, allowing you to take control of your thoughts and emotions and live your best life.

The cognitive triangle

The cognitive triangle is a fundamental concept in cognitive-behavioral therapy (CBT). It refers to the interconnectedness of our thoughts, emotions, and behavior. According to the cognitive triangle, our thoughts influence our emotions, which, in turn, influence our behavior. Conversely, our behavior can also affect our emotions and thoughts. This interconnectivity is the foundation of the CBT approach.

In the cognitive triangle, thoughts are considered the primary driver of emotions and behavior. The way we think about a situation determines how we feel and how we behave. For example, if we think of a situation as threatening or dangerous, we may feel anxious or fearful, and our behavior may be to avoid the situation. On the other hand, if we think of the same situation as manageable or even exciting, we may feel excited or motivated, and our behavior may be to approach the situation.

CBT therapists use the cognitive triangle to help clients identify and change negative thoughts that contribute to negative emotions and behavior. This process is known as cognitive restructuring. Clients learn to question their negative thoughts and replace them with more positive and realistic ones. For example, if a client has a negative thought like "I'm never going to be able to do this task," the therapist may ask them to challenge that thought by asking, "Is that really true? What evidence do you have to support that thought? Is there any evidence that contradicts it?" The client may then come up with a more positive thought like "I may struggle with this task, but I can break it down into smaller steps and ask for help if I need it."

The cognitive triangle also highlights the importance of behavior in CBT. Clients learn to identify behaviors that are maintaining their negative thoughts and emotions and to change those behaviors. For example, if a client is avoiding social situations because of social anxiety, the therapist may encourage them to gradually face their fears by attending social events in a step-by-step process.

In summary, the cognitive triangle is a powerful tool in CBT that helps clients understand the interconnectivity of their thoughts, emotions, and behavior. By identifying and changing negative thoughts and behaviors, clients can improve their emotional well-being and overall quality of life.

Challenging negative thoughts

Challenging Negative Thoughts

One of the core principles of cognitive-behavioral therapy (CBT) is recognizing and challenging negative thoughts. Negative thoughts can lead to negative emotions and behaviors, which can perpetuate a cycle of negativity and prevent us from achieving our goals and living fulfilling lives. In this subchapter, we will explore how to identify and challenge negative thoughts using CBT techniques.

Identifying Negative Thoughts

The first step in challenging negative thoughts is to become aware of them. Negative thoughts can be automatic and so ingrained in our thinking patterns that we may not even realize they are there. Common negative thoughts include:

- All-or-nothing thinking: Seeing things in black and white and not considering shades of gray.
- Overgeneralization: Making sweeping conclusions based on one or two incidents.
- Mind-reading: Assuming you know what others are thinking or feeling without evidence.
- Catastrophizing: Imagining the worst-case scenario.
- Personalization: Blaming yourself for things that are not your fault.

Once you have identified your negative thoughts, you can start to challenge them using the following CBT techniques.

Challenging Negative Thoughts

1. Rational questioning: Ask yourself if your negative thought is based on evidence or if it is just an assumption. For example, if you think, "I always mess things up," ask yourself if there is evidence to support this

belief. Have there been times when you did something well?

2. Alternative perspectives: Look for alternative explanations for the situation. For example, if your negative thought is, "My friend didn't call me back because she doesn't like me," consider other reasons why she might not have called, such as being busy or having a bad day.

3. Reality testing: Test the accuracy of your negative thought by gathering evidence. For example, if you think, "I'm not good at public speaking," challenge this thought by practicing and getting feedback from others.

4. Behavioral experiments: Test the validity of your negative thought by trying out new behaviors. For example, if you think, "I'm too anxious to go to a party," challenge this thought by going to the party and seeing how you feel.

By challenging negative thoughts with these CBT techniques, you can break the cycle of negativity and develop a more positive and realistic outlook on life. Practice these techniques regularly to develop a habit of challenging negative thoughts and living a more fulfilling life.

Relaxation techniques

Relaxation Techniques

Stress is an inevitable part of everyday life. It can be caused by various factors such as work pressure, relationship issues, financial problems, and health concerns. However, if not managed properly, stress can lead to anxiety, depression, and other mental health problems. This is where relaxation techniques come in handy.

Relaxation techniques are an effective way to manage stress and improve overall well-being. There are different types of relaxation techniques, and the goal is to find the one that works best for you. Here are some popular relaxation techniques:

1. Progressive Muscle Relaxation (PMR)

PMR involves tensing and relaxing different muscle groups in your body. You start by tensing the muscles in your feet and gradually move up to your head. This helps release tension and promote relaxation.

2. Deep Breathing

Deep breathing is a simple yet effective relaxation technique that involves taking slow, deep breaths. This helps slow down your heart rate and reduce stress.

3. Visualization

Visualization involves creating a mental image of a peaceful or calming scene. This could be a beach, a forest, or any other place that makes you feel relaxed.

4. Mindfulness

Mindfulness involves fully focusing on the present moment and observing your thoughts and feelings without judgment. This helps reduce stress and improve overall well-being.

5. Yoga

Yoga is a form of exercise that involves stretching, breathing, and relaxation techniques. It helps improve flexibility, reduce stress, and promote relaxation.

Incorporating relaxation techniques into your daily routine can help reduce stress and improve overall well-being. It is important to find the technique that works best for you and make it a part of your daily routine. With regular practice, you can achieve a sense of calm and relaxation even in the midst of a stressful situation.

THE CBT PROCESS

Setting goals

Setting Goals in CBT

One of the key components of Cognitive Behavioral Therapy (CBT) is setting goals. Goals are an important aspect of CBT because they provide a clear direction for therapy and help individuals to focus on what they want to achieve. Setting goals also helps to increase motivation and can provide a sense of accomplishment when they are achieved.

When setting goals in CBT, it is important to make them SMART goals. This means that they should be Specific, Measurable, Achievable, Relevant, and Time-bound. By making goals SMART, they are more likely to be achieved and progress can be tracked more easily.

To make a goal specific, it should be clear and concise. For example, instead of saying "I want to be happier", a specific goal would be "I want to increase my daily activities that bring me joy". Measurable goals allow for progress to be tracked. For example, instead of saying "I want to exercise more", a measurable goal would be "I want to walk for 30 minutes, three times a week".

Goals should also be achievable. It is important to set goals that are challenging but also realistic. For example, if someone has never exercised before, setting a goal to run a marathon in a month may not be achievable. Relevant goals are important because they relate to the individual's values and priorities. Finally, goals should be time-bound, meaning they have a specific date or time frame in which they should be achieved.

Once goals have been established, it is important to break them down into smaller, more manageable steps. This can help to prevent feeling overwhelmed and increase motivation. It is also important to anticipate and plan for potential challenges or obstacles that may arise during the process of achieving these goals.

Setting goals is an important part of CBT and can help individuals to achieve positive change in their lives. By making goals SMART and breaking them down into smaller steps, progress can be tracked and motivation can be increased.

Identifying negative thoughts

Identifying Negative Thoughts

Negative thoughts can be the root cause of many emotional and psychological problems that people face. In cognitive-behavioral therapy (CBT), identifying negative thoughts is the first step towards changing them. Negative thoughts can be categorized into different types, such as black and white thinking, catastrophizing, personalization, and overgeneralization.

Black and white thinking refers to thinking in extremes, where things are either all good or all bad. This kind of thinking can be harmful as it does not allow for any gray areas, leading to an unrealistic view of the world.

Catastrophizing is when someone imagines the worst-case scenario in any situation. This kind of thinking can lead to anxiety and depression, as the person is constantly worrying about things that may never happen.

Personalization is when someone takes things personally when they are not meant to be. This kind of thinking can lead to self-blame and self-criticism, which can be detrimental to one's mental health.

Overgeneralization is when a person takes one experience and applies it to all situations. This kind of thinking can lead to negative self-talk and a lack of confidence.

Identifying negative thoughts can be challenging, as they often happen automatically and unconsciously. However, with practice and awareness, it is possible to recognize negative thoughts and challenge them.

One technique used in CBT is to keep a thought diary, where the person writes down their thoughts and the situation that triggered them. This can help to identify patterns and themes in negative thinking.

Another technique is to question the validity of negative thoughts. This involves asking questions such as "Is this thought based on facts or assumptions?" and "What evidence do I have to support this thought?"

Challenging negative thoughts can be uncomfortable at first, but it is an essential step towards changing them. By identifying negative thoughts and challenging them, people can begin to reframe their thinking and improve their mental health.

In conclusion, identifying negative thoughts is an important step towards changing them in CBT. Negative thoughts can be categorized into different types, and techniques such as keeping a thought diary and questioning the validity of negative thoughts can be used to challenge them. By reframing negative thinking, people can improve their mental health and well-being.

Developing coping strategics

Developing Coping Strategies

Coping strategies are the tools we use to deal with life's challenges. These challenges can be anything from a difficult day at work to a major life event like a divorce or the death of a loved one. Coping strategies are essential for our mental well-being and can help us manage stress, anxiety, and depression.

CBT provides a range of coping strategies that can be used to help manage negative thoughts, feelings and behaviours. Here are some of the most commonly used coping strategies:

1. Mindfulness

Mindfulness is a technique that involves paying attention to the present moment without judgement. This can be done through meditation, breathing exercises or simply being aware of your surroundings. Mindfulness can help you stay focused and calm, and can help you manage stress and anxiety.

2. Relaxation Techniques

Relaxation techniques, such as progressive muscle relaxation or deep breathing, can help you reduce stress and anxiety. These techniques can be practiced regularly to help you manage your emotional state.

3. Cognitive Restructuring

Cognitive restructuring involves changing the way you think about a situation. This can help you to challenge negative thoughts and beliefs and replace them with more positive ones. This technique can help you to manage anxiety and depression.

4. Behavioural Activation

Behavioural activation involves increasing your level of activity and engagement in enjoyable activities. This can help you to feel more positive and motivated, and can help you to manage depression.

5. Problem-Solving

Problem-solving involves identifying a problem and coming up with a plan to solve it. This technique can help you to feel more in control and can help you to manage stress and anxiety.

In conclusion, developing coping strategies is an essential part of managing our mental well-being. CBT provides a range of coping strategies that can be used to help manage negative thoughts, feelings and behaviours. By implementing these strategies, you can take control of your mental health and improve your overall well-being.

Implementing coping strategies

Implementing Coping Strategies

When it comes to managing stress, anxiety, and depression, coping strategies play a critical role in helping individuals get through challenging times. Coping strategies refer to the behaviors and thoughts that people use to manage their emotions and deal with difficult situations. These strategies can be learned and developed through the practice of Cognitive Behavioral Therapy (CBT).

CBT is a powerful psychological intervention that helps individuals identify and change negative thought patterns and behaviors that contribute to their mental health issues. In this chapter, we will explore some of the most effective coping strategies that can be used to manage stress, anxiety, and depression.

1. Mindfulness Meditation

Mindfulness meditation is a powerful tool for managing stress and anxiety. It involves paying attention to your thoughts and feelings in a non-judgmental way. Mindfulness meditation helps individuals develop a sense of awareness and acceptance of their thoughts and feelings, which can ultimately lead to a sense of calm and inner peace.

2. Exercise

Exercise is a great way to manage stress and improve overall health and wellbeing. Exercise releases endorphins, which are natural mood boosters. It also helps individuals focus on something positive and gives them a sense of accomplishment.

3. Relaxation Techniques

Relaxation techniques such as deep breathing, progressive muscle relaxation, and visualization can be used to manage stress and anxiety. These techniques help individuals relax their muscles and calm their minds, which can reduce feelings of anxiety and tension.

4. Cognitive Restructuring

Cognitive restructuring is a key component of CBT. It involves identifying and challenging negative thought patterns that contribute to anxiety and depression. By changing the way individuals think about themselves and their situation, they can reduce their symptoms and improve their mental health.

5. Social Support

Social support is critical for managing stress and improving mental health. Having someone to talk to and share your feelings with can help individuals feel less alone and more supported. This can be a friend, family member, or therapist.

In conclusion, coping strategies are essential for managing stress, anxiety, and depression. By implementing these strategies into your daily routine, you can develop the skills and resilience needed to overcome any challenges that come your way. CBT is an effective way to learn and develop these coping strategies, and this book provides a comprehensive course in CBT that can help anyone improve their mental health and wellbeing.

Evaluating progress

Evaluating Progress

Evaluation is a crucial part of any CBT treatment plan. It is important to assess the progress of therapy to ensure that the treatment is effective and to make any necessary adjustments to the treatment plan. Evaluating progress can be done in several ways, including self-assessment, therapist evaluation, and feedback from others.

Self-Assessment

Self-assessment is a valuable tool for evaluating progress in CBT. Clients can keep track of their progress by completing regular assessments or questionnaires. These assessments can help clients identify their goals, assess their current functioning, and monitor their progress over time. Clients can also use self-monitoring techniques, such as keeping a journal, to track their thoughts, emotions, and behaviors. This can help clients identify patterns and triggers that may be contributing to their problems.

Therapist Evaluation

Therapist evaluation is another important tool for evaluating progress in CBT. Therapists can use a variety of methods to assess progress, such as standardized assessments or rating scales. They can also use clinical judgment and observations to evaluate progress. Therapists should regularly review treatment goals and progress with their clients to ensure that therapy is on track.

Feedback from Others

Feedback from others, such as family members or friends, can also be helpful in evaluating progress in CBT. Clients may not always be aware of changes in their behavior or functioning, but others may notice significant improvements. Feedback from others can also help clients identify areas for improvement and provide motivation to continue with treatment.

Overall, evaluating progress is an essential part of CBT treatment. Regular assessment and evaluation can help clients identify their goals, monitor their progress, and make any necessary adjustments to their treatment plan. Therapists should work collaboratively with their clients to ensure that treatment is effective and that progress is being made towards the client's goals.

COMMON CBT TECHNIQUES

Behavioral experiments

Behavioral experiments are a key component of Cognitive Behavioral Therapy (CBT) and involve testing beliefs and assumptions through real-life experiences. They are designed to challenge negative thoughts and beliefs that may be causing distress, anxiety, or depression. Behavioral experiments can help individuals to learn new ways of thinking and behaving that can improve their mental health and wellbeing.

The process of behavioral experiments involves setting up a hypothesis about a particular belief or assumption, testing it out in real-life situations, and then evaluating the results. For example, if someone has a fear of public speaking, they may have a belief that they will embarrass themselves in front of others. A behavioral experiment may involve giving a speech in front of a small group of people and then evaluating whether or not they actually embarrassed themselves.

The results of a behavioral experiment can help individuals to challenge their negative beliefs and assumptions. If the fear of public speaking was based on the belief that they would embarrass themselves, but the experiment showed that they did not, this can help to reduce anxiety and improve self-confidence.

Behavioral experiments can be used to test a wide range of beliefs and assumptions, from fears and phobias to negative self-talk and low self-esteem. They can be conducted in a variety of settings, such as at home, at work, or in social situations.

One of the benefits of behavioral experiments is that they are a practical and hands-on way of testing beliefs and assumptions. They allow individuals to see the results of their actions and to learn from their experiences. This can lead to a greater sense of self-awareness and an increased ability to manage emotions and behaviors.

In conclusion, behavioral experiments are a valuable tool in the CBT toolkit. They provide a practical and effective way of challenging negative beliefs and assumptions and can help individuals to develop new ways of thinking and behaving. By conducting behavioral experiments, individuals can improve their mental health and wellbeing, and ultimately lead more fulfilling lives.

Exposure therapy

Exposure therapy is a technique used in cognitive-behavioral therapy that involves exposing individuals to their fears or anxiety triggers in a safe and controlled environment. The goal of exposure therapy is to reduce the fear and anxiety associated with these triggers and help individuals develop coping mechanisms to manage their emotions.

Exposure therapy is based on the idea that avoidance of feared situations or triggers can actually reinforce anxiety and make it worse in the long run. By gradually exposing individuals to their fears, they can learn that their anxiety will eventually subside, and they can feel more in control of their emotions.

Exposure therapy can be used to treat a variety of anxiety disorders, including specific phobias, social anxiety, obsessive-compulsive disorder, and post-traumatic stress disorder. The therapist will work with the individual to create a hierarchy of feared situations or triggers, starting with the least anxiety-provoking and gradually working up to more challenging situations.

During exposure therapy, the individual may be asked to visualize or imagine the feared situation, or they may be exposed to it in real life. The therapist will guide them through the experience and help them develop coping strategies, such as deep breathing or positive self-talk.

It's important to note that exposure therapy should only be conducted by a trained professional, as it can be emotionally challenging and should be done in a safe and supportive environment. However, with proper guidance, exposure therapy can be an effective tool for managing anxiety and improving overall mental health.

In summary, exposure therapy is a technique used in cognitive-behavioral therapy to help individuals overcome their fears and anxiety. By gradually exposing individuals to their triggers in a safe and controlled environment, they can learn to manage their emotions and feel more in control of their mental health. If you are interested in learning more about exposure therapy, it's important to seek out a qualified therapist who can guide you through the process.

Thought records

Thought Records

One of the most effective techniques in cognitive-behavioral therapy (CBT) is thought records. This technique helps individuals identify and challenge negative thought patterns that can lead to negative emotions and behaviors. By learning to recognize these patterns and replace them with more realistic and positive ones, individuals can improve their mental health and increase their overall well-being.

What is a thought record?

A thought record is a tool used in CBT to help individuals identify and analyze their thoughts. It involves writing down a negative thought or belief and then examining it in more detail. The goal of a thought record is to help individuals identify the underlying beliefs and assumptions that are contributing to negative thoughts and emotions.

How to create a thought record

To create a thought record, follow these steps:

1. Identify the negative thought: Start by identifying the negative thought or belief that is causing distress. Write it down in as much detail as possible.

2. Examine the evidence: Look at the evidence for and against the negative thought. Is there any evidence to support it? Is there evidence to contradict it?

3. Challenge the thought: Ask yourself if the negative thought is logical and realistic. Is it based on facts or assumptions? What would you say to a friend who had the same thought?

4. Replace the negative thought: Once you have challenged the negative thought, replace it with a more realistic and positive one. Write down the new thought and how it makes you feel.

5. Repeat the process: Practice creating thought records regularly, especially when you are feeling distressed or anxious.

Benefits of using thought records

Using thought records can have several benefits, including:

- Improved self-awareness: By examining their thoughts and beliefs, individuals can gain a better understanding of their own thinking patterns and how they contribute to negative emotions.

- Increased self-esteem: By challenging negative thoughts and replacing them with positive ones, individuals can improve their self-esteem and confidence.

- Reduced anxiety and depression: Thought records can help individuals identify and challenge negative thought patterns that contribute to anxiety and depression.

In conclusion, thought records are a powerful tool in CBT that can help individuals identify and challenge negative thought patterns. By regularly practicing this technique, individuals can improve their mental health and increase their overall well-being.

Imagery techniques

Imagery techniques are powerful tools that can help individuals to visualize their fears and anxieties in a more manageable way. When used in Cognitive Behavioral Therapy (CBT), imagery techniques can help people to reframe their negative thoughts, reduce anxiety, and ultimately improve mental health.

One of the most common imagery techniques used in CBT is called imagery rescripting. This technique involves asking clients to imagine a traumatic or anxiety-provoking event from their past and then to change the outcome of that event in their mind. For example, if someone had a negative experience at a social gathering, they might be asked to imagine that same event but with a more positive outcome. This exercise can help to reduce the anxiety associated with the original event and empower individuals to take control of their thoughts and feelings.

Another imagery technique commonly used in CBT is visualization. Visualization involves asking clients to imagine themselves in a calm and peaceful environment, such as a beach or a forest. By visualizing this peaceful environment, individuals can learn to control their breathing and reduce their anxiety levels. Visualization can also be used to help individuals to imagine themselves successfully completing a task or overcoming a fear, which can be a powerful motivator for change.

Finally, guided imagery is another technique used in CBT that involves using audio recordings to guide individuals through a relaxation exercise. These recordings might include soothing music or the sound of a calming voice, and they can be used to help individuals to reduce their anxiety and improve their mental well-being.

Overall, imagery techniques can be incredibly effective tools in the treatment of anxiety and other mental health conditions. By using these techniques, individuals can learn to take control of their thoughts and feelings, reduce their anxiety levels, and ultimately improve their overall mental health and well-being.

Activity scheduling

Activity scheduling is an important component of cognitive-behavioral therapy that aims to help individuals develop a structured and fulfilling daily routine. It involves identifying activities that are important or enjoyable to the individual, scheduling them into their daily routine, and gradually increasing the amount of time spent on these activities.

The first step in activity scheduling is to identify activities that are important or enjoyable to the individual. This can include activities such as exercise, spending time with loved ones, pursuing hobbies, or engaging in relaxation techniques. The goal is to identify activities that provide a sense of pleasure or accomplishment, and that can be realistically incorporated into the individual's daily routine.

Once these activities have been identified, the next step is to schedule them into the individual's daily routine. This involves setting specific times during the day for each activity, and creating a structured daily schedule. It is important to start with small, manageable goals and gradually increase the amount of time spent on each activity.

Activity scheduling can be particularly helpful for individuals who are struggling with depression, anxiety, or other mental health conditions. It can help individuals regain a sense of control over their lives, increase their self-esteem and confidence, and reduce feelings of boredom or loneliness.

In addition to scheduling enjoyable or meaningful activities, it is also important to include activities that promote overall health and well-being. This can include activities such as exercise, healthy eating, and getting enough sleep.

Overall, activity scheduling is an important component of cognitive-behavioral therapy that can help individuals develop a structured and fulfilling daily routine. By identifying and scheduling enjoyable and meaningful activities, individuals can regain a sense of control over their lives, reduce feelings of boredom or loneliness, and promote overall health and well-being.

ADVANCED CBT TECHNIQUES

Mindfulness

Mindfulness is a powerful tool in the practice of Cognitive Behavioral Therapy (CBT). It is a technique that helps individuals focus on the present moment, accept their thoughts and feelings without judgment, and cultivate a sense of calmness and clarity. It is a crucial aspect of CBT that can help individuals break free from negative thought patterns and destructive behaviors.

The practice of mindfulness involves paying attention to the present moment and observing one's thoughts and emotions without judgment. By doing so, individuals can gain a deeper understanding of their mental processes and learn to respond to situations in a more constructive way. Mindfulness can help individuals break free from automatic negative thoughts and feelings, which can lead to anxiety, depression, and other mental health issues.

In CBT, mindfulness is often used in conjunction with other therapeutic techniques, such as cognitive restructuring and exposure therapy. By combining mindfulness with these techniques, individuals can learn to identify and challenge their negative thought patterns and develop more positive and adaptive ways of thinking.

There are many different ways to practice mindfulness, from traditional meditation practices to simple breathing exercises. One popular technique is called "mindful breathing," in which individuals focus on their breath and observe their thoughts and emotions as they arise. Other techniques include body scanning, progressive muscle relaxation, and visualization exercises.

While mindfulness can be a powerful tool in the practice of CBT, it is important to remember that it is not a quick fix or a cure-all. Like any therapeutic technique, it requires practice and patience to see results. However, with consistent practice, mindfulness can help individuals develop a more positive and healthy relationship with their thoughts and emotions, leading to greater overall well-being and mental health.

Acceptance and commitment therapy

Acceptance and Commitment Therapy, also known as ACT, is a form of cognitive-behavioral therapy that focuses on mindfulness and acceptance of one's thoughts and feelings. The main goal of ACT is to help individuals live a more meaningful and fulfilling life, even in the face of difficult thoughts and emotions.

ACT is based on six core principles: acceptance, cognitive defusion, being present in the moment, self-as-context, values, and committed action. Acceptance involves acknowledging and allowing difficult thoughts and emotions to exist without trying to change or control them. Cognitive defusion involves learning to observe thoughts without getting caught up in them. Being present in the moment involves focusing on the here and now, rather than dwelling on the past or worrying about the future. Self-as-context involves recognizing that we are more than our thoughts and feelings. Values involve identifying what is most important in our lives, and committed action involves taking steps toward those values, even in the face of difficult thoughts and emotions.

ACT can be helpful for a wide range of mental health concerns, including depression, anxiety, chronic pain, and substance abuse. It is particularly useful for individuals who have struggled with traditional forms of cognitive-behavioral therapy or who have found mindfulness practices helpful in the past.

If you are interested in learning more about ACT, there are a number of resources available. Many therapists are trained in ACT and can provide individual or group therapy. There are also a variety of self-help books and workbooks available that can guide you through the principles of ACT. Additionally, there are a number of online resources, including guided meditations and mindfulness exercises, that can help you incorporate ACT into your daily life.

Overall, ACT is a powerful tool for cultivating mindfulness and acceptance in the face of difficult thoughts and emotions. Whether you are struggling with a specific mental health concern or simply looking to live a more meaningful and fulfilling life, ACT can provide a valuable framework for growth and healing.

Dialectical behavior therapy

Dialectical behavior therapy (DBT) is a type of cognitive-behavioral therapy (CBT) that is designed to help individuals who struggle with intense and difficult-to-manage emotions. Developed by psychologist Marsha Linehan in the 1980s, DBT is a comprehensive treatment approach that incorporates a range of techniques and strategies to help clients build coping skills and improve their overall quality of life.

One of the key elements of DBT is its focus on mindfulness. This involves teaching clients how to be present in the moment, without judgment, and to develop an awareness of their thoughts, feelings, and physical sensations. By learning to be more mindful, individuals can better regulate their emotions and make more effective decisions.

Another important component of DBT is skills training. This involves teaching clients specific skills to help them manage their emotions and improve their relationships. These skills may include mindfulness, distress tolerance, emotion regulation, and interpersonal effectiveness.

In addition to skills training and mindfulness, DBT also incorporates individual therapy sessions and group therapy sessions. In individual therapy, clients work one-on-one with a therapist to address specific issues and develop personalized treatment goals. Group therapy, on the other hand, provides a supportive environment where clients can practice the skills they have learned and receive feedback from others who are going through similar experiences.

Overall, DBT is a highly effective form of CBT that has been shown to be particularly helpful for individuals who struggle with borderline personality disorder, as well as those with other mental health issues such as depression, anxiety, and substance abuse. With its focus on mindfulness, skills training, and supportive therapy, DBT provides a comprehensive approach to helping individuals manage their emotions and improve their overall well-being.

Schema therapy

Schema therapy is a form of cognitive-behavioral therapy that focuses on identifying and changing deeply ingrained patterns of thought and behavior. These patterns, known as schemas, are thought to develop early in life as a result of negative experiences and can continue to impact a person's life well into adulthood.

The goal of schema therapy is to help individuals identify their schemas and learn how to challenge and change them, ultimately leading to improved mental health and well-being. This therapy can be particularly helpful for individuals who struggle with long-standing emotional or relational issues, such as chronic depression, anxiety, or difficulty forming and maintaining close relationships.

One of the key components of schema therapy is the use of experiential techniques, such as imagery and role-playing, to help clients gain a deeper understanding of their schemas and how they impact their thoughts and behaviors. Through these techniques, clients are able to identify specific triggers that activate their schemas and learn new ways of responding in these situations.

Another important aspect of schema therapy is the focus on building a strong therapeutic relationship between client and therapist. This relationship is seen as essential to the success of the therapy, as it allows for a safe and supportive environment in which clients can explore their deepest fears and vulnerabilities.

Overall, schema therapy is a powerful tool for anyone seeking to understand and change deeply ingrained patterns of thought and behavior. Whether you're struggling with chronic emotional issues, or simply looking to improve your overall mental health and well-being, schema therapy can provide you with the tools and support you need to create lasting change in your life.

Cognitive restructuring

Cognitive restructuring is a key technique in cognitive-behavioral therapy (CBT) that helps individuals identify and challenge negative or irrational thoughts and beliefs, and replace them with more positive and realistic ones. This technique is based on the idea that our thoughts, emotions, and behaviors are interconnected, and that changing our thinking patterns can have a significant impact on how we feel and act.

The first step in cognitive restructuring is to identify the negative or irrational thoughts that are causing distress or interfering with daily functioning. These may include automatic negative thoughts (ANTs) such as "I'm a failure," or "No one likes me," as well as cognitive distortions or thinking errors such as black-and-white thinking or overgeneralization.

Once these thoughts have been identified, the next step is to challenge them using evidence-based reasoning. This involves examining the evidence for and against the negative thought, and considering alternative explanations or perspectives. For example, if someone is struggling with the thought "I'll never be able to do this," they might challenge this thought by asking themselves questions such as "What evidence do I have to support this thought?" and "What evidence do I have to contradict this thought?"

The final step in cognitive restructuring is to replace the negative thought with a more positive and realistic one. This might involve developing coping statements or affirmations that counteract the negative thought, such as "I can do this with practice and hard work," or "I am worthy of love and respect."

Cognitive restructuring is a powerful tool for overcoming negative thinking patterns and improving overall mental health and well-being. By challenging and replacing negative thoughts with more positive and realistic ones, individuals can reduce anxiety and depression, increase self-esteem, and improve their ability to cope with life's challenges.

APPLYING CBT TO SPECIFIC ISSUES

Anxiety disorders

Anxiety Disorders

Anxiety disorders are among the most common mental health conditions faced by individuals today. It is characterized by feelings of excessive worry, fear, or apprehension in response to stressful or intimidating situations. These feelings can be so overwhelming that they can interfere with daily activities, social relationships, and overall quality of life.

Fortunately, cognitive-behavioral therapy (CBT) offers effective treatment for anxiety disorders. CBT is a form of psychotherapy that focuses on changing negative thought patterns and behaviors that contribute to anxiety. This therapy aims to help individuals learn new skills and strategies to manage their symptoms and improve their quality of life.

There are several types of anxiety disorders, including generalized anxiety disorder, panic disorder, social anxiety disorder, and specific phobias. Each of these disorders has its unique symptoms and treatment strategies. However, the core principles of CBT remain the same.

The first step in CBT for anxiety disorders is to identify the negative thought patterns that contribute to anxiety. These thoughts are often irrational and unrealistic, and they create a cycle of anxiety and worry. The therapist works with the individual to identify these thoughts and replace them with more realistic and positive ones.

The next step is to learn coping strategies to manage anxiety symptoms. This may include relaxation techniques, such as deep breathing and progressive muscle relaxation, as well as exposure therapy. Exposure therapy involves gradually exposing the individual to the situation or object that triggers anxiety, in a safe and controlled environment. This helps the individual to confront their fears and develop confidence in their ability to manage anxiety.

CBT also involves behavioral techniques to address anxiety. This includes setting achievable goals and rewarding oneself for progress. It also involves developing a routine that promotes a healthy lifestyle, including regular exercise, healthy eating, and adequate sleep.

In conclusion, anxiety disorders can be debilitating, but they are treatable. CBT offers a comprehensive approach to managing anxiety symptoms and improving overall quality of life. With the right skills and strategies, individuals can learn to manage their anxiety and live a more fulfilling life.

Depression

Depression is a common mental health condition that affects millions of people worldwide. It is a serious illness that can have a profound impact on an individual's quality of life, relationships, and overall well-being. Depression is characterized by persistent feelings of sadness, hopelessness, and a lack of interest in daily activities. It can also cause physical symptoms such as fatigue, sleep disturbances, and appetite changes.

Cognitive-behavioral therapy (CBT) is an effective treatment for depression. It is a type of talk therapy that focuses on identifying and changing negative thought patterns and behaviors that contribute to depression. CBT teaches individuals skills to manage their symptoms, improve their mood, and feel more in control of their lives.

One of the first steps in treating depression with CBT is to identify negative thought patterns. These are often automatic thoughts that occur without conscious awareness. Examples of negative thoughts include "I'm a failure," "Nothing ever goes right for me," or "I'm not good enough." These thoughts can be irrational and unhelpful, but they can have a powerful impact on an individual's mood and behavior.

Once negative thoughts have been identified, CBT teaches individuals to challenge them. This involves questioning the evidence for the negative thought, considering alternative explanations, and evaluating the accuracy of the thought. For example, if someone is thinking "I'm a failure," they may ask themselves, "What evidence do I have to support this thought? What evidence do I have that contradicts this thought?"

CBT also teaches individuals to develop more positive and realistic thoughts to replace negative ones. This can involve creating a list of positive affirmations or using positive self-talk to counteract negative thoughts. For example, instead of thinking "I'm a failure," someone might replace this thought with "I'm not perfect, but I'm doing my best."

In addition to changing negative thought patterns, CBT also focuses on changing behaviors that contribute to depression. This can involve setting goals and developing a plan to achieve them, engaging in pleasurable activities, and practicing relaxation techniques.

Overall, CBT is a comprehensive and effective treatment for depression. It helps individuals learn skills to manage their symptoms, improve their mood, and feel more in control of their lives. With practice and commitment, CBT can help individuals break free from the cycle of depression and live a happier, healthier life.

Obsessive-compulsive disorder

Obsessive-compulsive disorder, or OCD, is a mental health condition that affects millions of people worldwide. It is characterized by persistent and intrusive thoughts, images, or impulses (obsessions) that cause significant distress or anxiety, and repetitive behaviors or mental acts (compulsions) that are performed to alleviate this distress or prevent harm or danger. OCD can interfere with a person's daily functioning, relationships, and quality of life if left untreated.

The exact causes of OCD are still not fully understood, but research suggests that it may be related to a combination of genetic, neurological, and environmental factors. Some common OCD themes include contamination and cleanliness, symmetry and order, harm or danger, and sexual or religious obsessions. Compulsions can take many forms, such as washing, checking, counting, arranging, or seeking reassurance.

Cognitive-behavioral therapy (CBT) is an evidence-based treatment for OCD that combines cognitive restructuring, exposure and response prevention (ERP), and other techniques to help individuals overcome their symptoms and improve their functioning. CBT for OCD typically involves several stages, including psychoeducation, assessment, goal-setting, treatment planning, and maintenance.

The first step in CBT for OCD is to help individuals understand the nature of their condition and how it affects their thoughts, feelings, and behaviors. This may involve explaining the cognitive model of OCD, which emphasizes the role of distorted beliefs and appraisals in maintaining the cycle of obsessions and compulsions. It may also involve identifying and challenging negative automatic thoughts and core beliefs that contribute to OCD.

The next step is to conduct a thorough assessment of the individual's OCD symptoms, triggers, and underlying factors. This may involve using standardized measures, conducting interviews, and gathering information from family members or other sources. The assessment helps to inform the treatment plan and identify specific targets for intervention.

The core component of CBT for OCD is ERP, which involves gradually exposing the individual to feared situations or stimuli while preventing them from engaging in compulsive behaviors or mental acts. ERP is based on the principle of habituation, which suggests that repeated exposure to anxiety-provoking stimuli can lead to a decrease in anxiety over time. ERP can be challenging and uncomfortable, but it is highly effective in reducing OCD symptoms and improving quality of life.

Other techniques that may be used in CBT for OCD include mindfulness, cognitive restructuring, problem-solving, and relapse prevention. Mindfulness can help individuals to increase awareness of their thoughts and emotions without judging or reacting to them. Cognitive restructuring involves identifying and challenging cognitive distortions and replacing them with more realistic and adaptive thoughts. Problem-solving can help individuals to develop effective coping strategies for dealing with stressors and challenges. Relapse prevention involves creating a plan for maintaining gains and preventing relapse after treatment.

In conclusion, OCD is a common and debilitating mental health condition that can be effectively treated with CBT. CBT for OCD involves several stages, including psychoeducation, assessment, goal-setting, treatment planning, and maintenance. The core component of CBT for OCD is ERP, which involves gradually exposing the individual to feared situations or stimuli while preventing them from engaging in compulsive behaviors or mental acts. Other techniques that may be used in CBT for

OCD include mindfulness, cognitive restructuring, problem-solving, and relapse prevention. With the help of a qualified CBT therapist and a commitment to treatment, individuals with OCD can overcome their symptoms and improve their quality of life.

Post-traumatic stress disorder

Post-traumatic stress disorder (PTSD) is a mental health condition that can occur after someone has experienced or witnessed a traumatic event. These events can range from natural disasters to violent incidents, and can cause a range of symptoms that can interfere with daily life. PTSD can affect anyone, regardless of age, gender, or background.

Symptoms of PTSD can include flashbacks, nightmares, feelings of detachment, and avoidance of triggers that remind the person of the traumatic event. These symptoms can make it difficult to function in daily life, and can lead to depression, anxiety, and other mental health problems.

Cognitive-behavioral therapy (CBT) is an effective treatment for PTSD. CBT focuses on changing negative thought patterns and behaviors that can be associated with PTSD. This type of therapy can be done individually or in group settings, and may involve a combination of techniques such as exposure therapy, cognitive restructuring, and relaxation techniques.

Exposure therapy involves gradually exposing the person to the triggers that cause their PTSD symptoms, such as loud noises or crowded spaces. This exposure is done in a controlled environment, and the therapist helps the person learn coping skills to manage their anxiety and fear.

Cognitive restructuring involves identifying and changing negative thought patterns that are associated with the traumatic event. This can involve challenging beliefs about the event or themselves, and replacing them with more positive and realistic thoughts.

Relaxation techniques can help manage the physical symptoms of anxiety that can be associated with PTSD. These techniques can include deep breathing exercises, progressive muscle relaxation, and mindfulness meditation.

CBT is a highly effective treatment for PTSD, and can help individuals regain control over their lives and reduce their symptoms. It is important to seek treatment for PTSD as soon as possible, as symptoms can worsen over time if left untreated. If you or someone you know is experiencing symptoms of PTSD, don't hesitate to seek help from a mental health professional.

Eating disorders

Eating disorders are a group of conditions that involve abnormal eating habits and severe distress or concern about body weight or shape. They can be life-threatening if left untreated, making it essential to address them as soon as possible.

The most common types of eating disorders are anorexia nervosa, bulimia nervosa, and binge-eating disorder. Anorexia nervosa is characterized by extreme weight loss, a distorted body image, and an intense fear of gaining weight. Bulimia nervosa involves a cycle of binge eating followed by purging, such as self-induced vomiting or the use of laxatives. Binge-eating disorder is characterized by episodes of excessive eating, often followed by feelings of guilt or shame.

Cognitive-behavioral therapy (CBT) can be an effective treatment for eating disorders. CBT focuses on changing negative thoughts and behaviors that contribute to the eating disorder. It can also help individuals develop healthy coping mechanisms and improve their self-esteem.

In CBT for eating disorders, the therapist works with the individual to identify and challenge negative thoughts and beliefs about food, weight, and body image. They may also use exposure therapy to gradually expose the individual to feared foods or situations, helping them to develop more positive associations with them.

CBT can also help individuals develop healthy eating habits and improve their relationship with food. This may involve creating a meal plan, setting realistic goals, and learning how to manage cravings and urges.

In addition to CBT, other treatments for eating disorders may include medication, family therapy, and nutritional counseling. It's important to work with a healthcare professional to determine the best course of treatment for each individual.

Overall, eating disorders can be challenging to overcome, but with the right treatment and support, recovery is possible. CBT can be a valuable tool in addressing the negative thoughts and behaviors that contribute to these conditions and helping individuals develop a healthier relationship with food and their bodies.

CBT AND RELATIONSHIPS

Communication skills

Communication skills are an essential aspect of cognitive-behavioral therapy (CBT). They play a crucial role in building strong relationships, expressing oneself effectively, and managing conflicts. In this chapter, we will explore the importance of communication skills in CBT and how to develop them to enhance our therapeutic outcomes.

Effective communication is a two-way process that involves both speaking and listening skills. In CBT, therapists use various communication skills to help clients identify and modify their negative thoughts and behaviors. They also teach clients how to communicate assertively, express their emotions, and negotiate conflicts.

One of the essential communication skills in CBT is active listening. Active listening involves paying attention to what the client is saying, both verbally and nonverbally. It also involves demonstrating empathy, asking clarifying questions, and summarizing what the client has said. Active listening helps the therapist to understand the client's perspective and build a strong therapeutic alliance.

Another important communication skill is assertiveness. Assertive communication involves expressing oneself in a clear, direct, and respectful manner. It involves being able to say no, express one's needs and feelings, and negotiate conflicts. Assertive communication can help clients to improve their self-esteem, reduce anxiety, and build healthier relationships.

In CBT, therapists also use communication skills to facilitate problem-solving and decision-making. They teach clients how to brainstorm solutions, weigh the pros and cons of different options, and make informed choices. Effective communication can help clients to overcome their negative thoughts and behaviors and achieve their goals.

Finally, communication skills are essential in maintaining the therapeutic relationship. Therapists must be able to communicate boundaries, expectations, and feedback to clients in a clear and respectful manner. Effective communication can help clients to trust their therapist, feel heard and understood, and achieve their therapeutic goals.

In conclusion, communication skills are an essential aspect of cognitive-behavioral therapy. They play a crucial role in building strong relationships, expressing oneself effectively, and managing conflicts. In this chapter, we have explored the importance of communication skills in CBT and how to develop them to enhance our therapeutic outcomes. By improving our communication skills, we can help clients to overcome their negative thoughts and behaviors and achieve their goals.

Conflict resolution

Conflict resolution is an essential life skill that everyone should have. It involves the ability to identify, manage, and resolve conflicts in a constructive and positive manner. Conflict can arise in any situation, whether at work, home, or in social settings. The key to successful conflict resolution is to approach the situation with an open mind, a willingness to listen and understand the other person's perspective, and a commitment to finding a solution that is acceptable to all parties involved.

Cognitive-behavioral therapy (CBT) can be an effective tool for conflict resolution. CBT is a psychotherapeutic approach that focuses on changing negative thought patterns and behavior that contribute to emotional distress. It can be used to help individuals identify and modify their thoughts and behaviors related to conflict, leading to more positive outcomes.

One of the first steps in conflict resolution is to identify the source of the conflict. This can involve asking questions to clarify the issues and concerns of all parties involved. Once the source of the conflict has been identified, it is important to communicate effectively. This involves active listening and expressing oneself in a clear and respectful manner.

CBT can be used to address cognitive distortions that contribute to conflict. For example, individuals may have negative thoughts about themselves, others, or the situation that can escalate the conflict. Through CBT, individuals can learn to identify and challenge these negative thoughts, leading to more positive and productive interactions.

Another important aspect of conflict resolution is finding a solution that is acceptable to all parties involved. This may involve compromise or finding a creative solution that meets everyone's needs. CBT can be used to help individuals develop problem-solving skills and to approach conflict in a more rational and constructive manner.

In conclusion, conflict resolution is an essential life skill that can be improved through the use of cognitive-behavioral therapy. By identifying the source of the conflict, communicating effectively, and finding a solution that is acceptable to all parties involved, individuals can resolve conflicts in a positive and productive manner.

Building healthy relationships

Building Healthy Relationships

Relationships are an integral part of our lives, and they can be a source of both joy and stress. Whether it is a romantic relationship, a friendship, or a professional connection, building and maintaining healthy relationships is essential for our wellbeing.

In this chapter, we will explore how Cognitive Behavioral Therapy (CBT) can help us build and maintain healthy relationships. We will discuss the common problems that can arise in relationships, the cognitive and behavioral factors that contribute to these problems, and the strategies we can use to overcome them.

Common Relationship Problems

Relationship problems can take many forms, such as communication breakdowns, conflicts, and misunderstandings. These problems can arise due to a variety of factors, including:

- Negative thinking patterns: Negative thoughts and beliefs about ourselves, our partners, or the relationship can lead to misunderstandings, conflicts, and emotional distress.
- Poor communication: Communication is a crucial element of any relationship, and poor communication can lead to misunderstandings, conflicts, and feelings of resentment.

- Unhealthy behaviors: Behaviors such as criticism, blaming, and defensiveness can create a negative cycle in relationships, leading to further problems.

CBT Strategies for Building Healthy Relationships

CBT offers several strategies that can help us build and maintain healthy relationships. These strategies include:

1. Identifying and challenging negative thoughts: By identifying and challenging negative thoughts about ourselves, our partners, or the relationship, we can reduce the impact of these thoughts on our emotions and behavior.

2. Practicing effective communication: Effective communication involves active listening, expressing ourselves clearly and assertively, and avoiding negative communication patterns such as criticism and defensiveness.

3. Developing empathy: Empathy involves understanding and sharing the feelings of

others. By developing empathy, we can improve our relationships by showing understanding and support.

4. Setting boundaries: Setting boundaries involves establishing clear limits on what is acceptable behavior in a relationship. By setting boundaries, we can protect ourselves from unhealthy behaviors and maintain healthy relationships.

Conclusion

Building healthy relationships requires effort and commitment, but it is essential for our wellbeing. By using CBT strategies such as identifying and challenging negative thoughts, practicing effective communication, developing empathy, and setting boundaries, we can overcome common relationship problems and build strong, healthy relationships.

Addressing codependency

Addressing Codependency

Codependency is a complex issue that affects many people. It is a term that describes a dysfunctional relationship where one person enables or supports the other person's unhealthy behaviors or addiction. Codependency can occur in any type of relationship, including romantic relationships, friendships, and family relationships. It is often difficult for people to recognize codependency in their own relationships, and even more challenging to overcome it. However, by applying the principles of Cognitive Behavioral Therapy (CBT), it is possible to address codependency and improve the quality of your relationships.

One of the key features of codependency is a lack of boundaries. This means that the codependent person often puts the needs of others before their own, and struggles to say no. This can lead to feelings of resentment and frustration, as well as an inability to take care of oneself. To address codependency, it is important to identify your own needs and set clear boundaries with others. This may involve learning how to say no, and also learning how to communicate your needs effectively.

Another important aspect of addressing codependency is developing a strong sense of self-worth. Codependent people often base their self-worth on the approval of others, which can lead to feelings of inadequacy and low self-esteem. By learning to value yourself for who you are, rather than what others think of you, you can improve your self-esteem and reduce your reliance on others for validation.

CBT can also be helpful in addressing the underlying beliefs and thoughts that contribute to codependency. For example, many codependent people have a belief that they must take care of others in order to be loved and accepted. By challenging these beliefs and replacing them with more realistic and healthy thoughts, you can begin to break the cycle of codependency.

In conclusion, addressing codependency is a challenging but important process that can greatly improve the quality of your relationships and your overall well-being. By applying the principles of CBT, you can learn to set boundaries, develop a strong sense of self-worth, and challenge the underlying beliefs and thoughts that contribute to codependency. With time and practice, you can break free from codependency and enjoy healthier, more fulfilling relationships.

CBT AND SELF-CARE

Self-esteem

Self-esteem is a critical component of our mental health, and it plays a vital role in determining our overall level of happiness and well-being. People with high self-esteem typically have a positive outlook on life, are more confident, and are better equipped to handle challenges and setbacks.

On the other hand, people with low self-esteem tend to have negative thoughts and beliefs about themselves, which can lead to feelings of worthlessness, anxiety, and depression. Low self-esteem can also make it more difficult to form positive relationships, pursue personal goals, and achieve success in various areas of life.

Fortunately, Cognitive Behavioral Therapy (CBT) offers effective strategies for improving self-esteem and developing a more positive self-image. In this chapter, we will explore some of the key concepts and techniques used in CBT to help individuals improve their self-esteem.

One of the first things to understand about self-esteem is that it is not fixed or static. Instead, it fluctuates based on our thoughts, beliefs, and experiences. CBT helps individuals identify and challenge negative self-talk and beliefs that contribute to low self-esteem.

CBT also emphasizes the importance of setting realistic goals and focusing on personal strengths and achievements. By identifying areas of competency and success, individuals can build a foundation of positive self-esteem and begin to challenge negative self-perceptions.

Another critical aspect of self-esteem is self-care. CBT encourages individuals to prioritize self-care practices that improve physical and mental health, such as regular exercise, healthy eating, and getting enough rest. By taking care of ourselves, we signal to our brains that we are worth investing in, which can help boost self-esteem.

Finally, CBT helps individuals develop more positive self-talk and affirmations. By consciously replacing negative self-talk with positive affirmations, individuals can begin to reshape their self-perception and improve their self-esteem.

In summary, self-esteem is a critical component of our mental health, and CBT offers effective strategies for improving self-esteem and developing a more positive self-image. By challenging negative self-talk, focusing on personal strengths and achievements, prioritizing self-care, and developing positive self-talk, individuals can build a foundation of positive self-esteem and achieve greater happiness and well-being.

Stress management

Stress Management

Stress is a common issue that affects many people, and it can have a significant negative impact on mental health and well-being. Stress can be caused by a variety of factors, such as work, relationships, finances, and health problems. Fortunately, there are effective strategies for managing stress, and cognitive-behavioral therapy (CBT) can be a powerful tool for reducing stress levels.

CBT can help individuals identify and challenge negative thought patterns that contribute to stress. By changing the way you think about stressful situations, you can reduce the intensity of your emotional response and feel more in control. CBT can also teach you coping skills to manage stress more effectively, such as relaxation techniques, time management strategies, and problem-solving skills.

One effective CBT technique for managing stress is called cognitive restructuring. This technique involves identifying and challenging negative thoughts and replacing them with more positive and realistic ones. For example, if you find yourself thinking, "I can't handle this," you can challenge that thought by asking yourself, "What evidence do I have that I can't handle this?" and "What are some other ways I could approach this situation?" By reframing your thoughts in a more positive and realistic way, you can reduce the amount of stress you experience.

Another CBT technique for managing stress is relaxation training. This involves learning to relax your body and mind through techniques such as deep breathing, progressive muscle relaxation, and visualization. By practicing relaxation techniques regularly, you can reduce the physical symptoms of stress and feel more calm and centered.

CBT can also teach you strategies for managing your time more effectively, which can reduce stress levels. For example, you can learn to prioritize tasks, set realistic goals, and break large projects into smaller, more manageable tasks. By becoming more organized and efficient, you can reduce the amount of stress you experience and feel more in control of your life.

In conclusion, stress can be a significant challenge, but there are effective strategies for managing it. CBT can be a powerful tool for reducing stress levels by helping you identify and challenge negative thought patterns, teaching you coping skills, and helping you manage your time more effectively. By incorporating these techniques into your daily routine, you can reduce stress levels and improve your overall well-being.

Assertiveness

Assertiveness is a crucial life skill that everyone should possess. It refers to the ability to express your needs, wants, and opinions in a clear and confident manner without infringing on the rights of others. Assertiveness is not about being aggressive or dominating but rather about being self-assured and respectful to others. It is an essential component of Cognitive Behavioral Therapy (CBT) as it helps individuals to communicate effectively and assertively in their daily lives.

Many people struggle with assertiveness, either by being too passive or too aggressive. Passive individuals often have a hard time expressing themselves and standing up for their needs, while aggressive individuals may violate the rights of others in their efforts to get what they want. The goal of CBT is to help individuals develop a healthy balance between assertiveness and flexibility.

Assertiveness training is a vital component of CBT, and it involves teaching individuals how to express their feelings, thoughts, and needs in a clear and direct manner. They learn how to communicate effectively while maintaining respect for themselves and others. The training may include role-playing exercises, assertiveness rehearsal, and cognitive restructuring. The purpose is to help individuals overcome the fear of expressing themselves, develop self-confidence, and learn to handle conflicts constructively.

Assertiveness is not just about verbal communication, but also about body language and tone of voice. In CBT, individuals learn to be aware of their non-verbal communication and how it can affect their assertiveness. They also learn to use positive self-talk to enhance their self-confidence, overcome negative thoughts, and reduce anxiety.

Assertiveness is a skill that can be learned and developed through CBT. It is essential for building healthy relationships, setting boundaries, and achieving personal goals. By learning to be assertive, individuals can improve their self-esteem, reduce stress, and enhance their overall well-being. CBT provides a comprehensive course in assertiveness training that enables individuals to communicate effectively and assertively in their daily lives.

Time management

Time management is an essential skill that is often overlooked when it comes to self-care and mental health. In the context of cognitive-behavioral therapy (CBT), it is crucial to learn how to manage your time effectively to reduce stress and anxiety, increase productivity, and improve overall well-being.

The first step in effective time management is to identify your goals and priorities. This involves setting realistic and achievable goals, both short-term and long-term. By doing this, you can prioritize your tasks and activities based on their importance and relevance to your goals. It is also essential to break down larger tasks into smaller, more manageable ones to avoid feeling overwhelmed.

Another key aspect of time management is to develop a routine or schedule that works for you. This involves allocating specific times for tasks, such as work or study, exercise, socializing, and relaxation. By having a set routine, you can create a sense of structure and predictability in your day, which can help reduce stress and increase focus.

Effective time management also involves learning how to say no to tasks or activities that do not align with your goals or priorities. This can be challenging, especially if you are used to saying yes to everything. However, learning to set boundaries and prioritize your time can help reduce stress and increase productivity.

CBT also emphasizes the importance of self-awareness in time management. This involves paying attention to your thoughts and feelings in relation to your time management skills. For example, if you find yourself consistently procrastinating or struggling to stick to a routine, it may be helpful to explore any underlying beliefs or attitudes that may be contributing to these behaviors.

Overall, effective time management is an essential skill for anyone looking to improve their mental health and well-being. By setting goals, developing a routine, learning to say no, and practicing self-awareness, you can reduce stress, increase productivity, and achieve your goals.

CBT AND PERSONAL GROWTH

Identifying values

Identifying Values

Identifying your values is a crucial component of cognitive-behavioral therapy (CBT). Values are the guiding principles that give meaning and purpose to our lives. They are the things that we hold dear and strive for, whether it be love, family, happiness, success, or personal growth.

In CBT, identifying your values is important because it helps you to understand what is truly important to you. Once you have a clear understanding of your values, you can use them to guide your decision-making and behavior. This is because when your actions align with your values, you will feel a sense of fulfillment and satisfaction.

To identify your values, you can start by asking yourself some key questions such as:

- What is important to me in life?
- What do I want to achieve in life?
- What are my long-term goals?
- What makes me happy?

Once you have identified your values, it is important to prioritize them. This means identifying which values are most important to you and which values are less important. Prioritizing your values will help you to focus on what truly matters and make decisions that align with your most important values.

It is important to note that values can change over time. As you grow and experience new things, your values may shift. It is important to regularly reassess your values and make adjustments as needed.

Identifying your values is an important step in the CBT process. By understanding what is most important to you, you can make decisions and take actions that align with your values and ultimately lead to a more fulfilling life.

Goal setting

Goal Setting: A Key Component of CBT

Goal setting is one of the most important components of Cognitive Behavioral Therapy (CBT). The process of setting goals in CBT is designed to help individuals identify and work towards specific objectives that can lead to improvements in their mental health and wellbeing.

There are several reasons why goal setting is so important in CBT. First, setting goals can help individuals gain a sense of control over their lives. When someone has a clear goal in mind, they are more likely to feel motivated and empowered to take action towards achieving that goal.

Second, goal setting can help individuals break down larger, more daunting problems into smaller, more manageable pieces. This can make it easier to take concrete steps towards finding solutions to these problems.

Finally, goal setting can help individuals track their progress over time. By setting specific, measurable goals, individuals can see how far they have come and celebrate their achievements along the way.

When setting goals in CBT, it is important to keep a few key principles in mind. First, goals should be specific and measurable. This means that they should be clearly defined and there should be some way to track progress towards achieving them.

Second, goals should be realistic and achievable. While it is important to set ambitious goals, it is also important to make sure that they are within reach. Setting unattainable goals can lead to feelings of frustration and disappointment, which can undermine progress towards achieving them.

Third, goals should be relevant to the individual's values and priorities. In other words, goals should be aligned with what is most important to the individual in their life. When goals are aligned with values and priorities, individuals are more likely to feel motivated and committed to achieving them.

Finally, goals should be time-bound. This means that there should be a specific deadline for achieving each goal. This helps to create a sense of urgency and can help individuals stay focused and motivated over time.

Overall, goal setting is a key component of CBT that can help individuals gain a sense of control over their lives, break down larger problems into manageable pieces, track progress over time, and achieve meaningful improvements in their mental health and wellbeing. By following these key principles of goal setting, individuals can set themselves up for success and achieve their most important objectives.

Overcoming obstacles

Overcoming obstacles is a fundamental aspect of cognitive-behavioral therapy (CBT). It is a process of identifying and addressing the challenges that prevent individuals from achieving their goals and living fulfilling lives. CBT teaches individuals to develop problem-solving skills and to manage their thoughts and behaviors in a more effective way.

One of the most common obstacles that individuals face is negative thinking patterns. Negative thinking can lead to feelings of anxiety, depression, and hopelessness. CBT helps individuals to identify negative thought patterns and to challenge them with evidence-based reasoning. This process helps individuals to develop a more positive and realistic outlook on life.

Another obstacle that individuals face is avoidance. Avoidance can take many forms, including avoiding social situations, work, or school. CBT teaches individuals to face their fears and to gradually expose themselves to the situations that they have been avoiding. This process helps individuals to develop coping skills and to overcome their fears.

CBT also addresses the obstacles of low self-esteem and self-criticism. Low self-esteem can lead to feelings of worthlessness and can prevent individuals from achieving their goals. CBT helps individuals to develop a more positive self-image and to challenge negative self-talk. This process helps individuals to develop self-compassion and to achieve their full potential.

Finally, CBT addresses the obstacles of stress and anxiety. Stress and anxiety can be overwhelming and can interfere with daily life. CBT helps individuals to develop relaxation techniques and to manage their stress and anxiety in a more effective way. This process helps individuals to feel more in control of their lives and to achieve a greater sense of well-being.

In conclusion, overcoming obstacles is a key component of CBT. By identifying and addressing the challenges that prevent individuals from achieving their goals, CBT helps individuals to develop problem-solving skills, to manage their thoughts and behaviors, and to achieve a greater sense of well-being.

Achieving success

Achieving Success

Success means different things to different people. However, for most people, success is about achieving their goals and feeling satisfied with their lives. CBT can be an effective tool for achieving success, whether it is in personal, professional, or academic endeavors.

CBT helps people identify and modify negative thoughts and behaviors that might be hindering their success. By recognizing their negative patterns, individuals can replace them with more positive and productive ones. This can lead to increased confidence, motivation, and a greater sense of control over one's life.

One key to achieving success with CBT is setting realistic and achievable goals. Goals should be specific, measurable, and time-bound. This means that they should be clearly defined, quantifiable, and have a deadline. For example, a goal of "improving my grades" is vague and difficult to measure, whereas a goal of "achieving a B+ or higher in all of my classes this semester" is specific and measurable.

Another important aspect of achieving success with CBT is developing healthy coping mechanisms. This involves learning to manage stress and difficult emotions in a constructive way. Some effective coping strategies include deep breathing, mindfulness meditation, exercise, and talking to a trusted friend or therapist.

CBT can also help individuals overcome obstacles that might be preventing them from achieving success. For example, if someone is struggling with procrastination, CBT can help them identify the underlying reasons for their behavior and develop strategies to overcome it. This might involve breaking tasks down into smaller, more manageable steps, setting deadlines, and rewarding oneself for completing tasks on time.

In conclusion, CBT can be a powerful tool for achieving success in all areas of life. By setting realistic goals, developing healthy coping mechanisms, and overcoming obstacles, individuals can build the skills and confidence they need to achieve their dreams. With dedication and commitment, anyone can use CBT to reach their full potential and live a fulfilling life.

CONCLUSION

The benefits of completing a CBT course in a single book

The benefits of completing a CBT course in a single book are numerous. Firstly, it is an incredibly efficient way to learn the principles and techniques of cognitive behavioral therapy. Instead of having to attend weekly sessions with a therapist or take an online course with multiple modules, you can get everything you need to know from one comprehensive book.

Another advantage of completing a CBT course in a single book is that it is cost-effective. Attending therapy sessions can be expensive, and online courses often require monthly subscriptions or additional fees for certification. With a single book, you have a one-time cost that will give you a lifetime of knowledge and skills.

Additionally, completing a CBT course in a single book allows you to work at your own pace. You can read through the material as quickly or as slowly as you need to, taking the time to fully understand each concept before moving on to the next. This is especially helpful for people who may not have the time to commit to a weekly therapy session or online course.

Another benefit of completing a CBT course in a single book is the flexibility it provides. You can take the book with you wherever you go, allowing you to read and practice the techniques whenever you have free time. This is especially helpful for people who travel frequently or have busy schedules.

Finally, completing a CBT course in a single book can be empowering. You are taking control of your own mental health and learning skills that can help you manage your thoughts and emotions more effectively. This can lead to increased self-confidence and a sense of accomplishment.

In conclusion, completing a CBT course in a single book is an efficient, cost-effective, flexible, and empowering way to learn the principles and techniques of cognitive behavioral therapy. Whether you are struggling with anxiety, depression, or simply want to improve your mental well-being, a comprehensive CBT course in a single book can provide you with the tools you need to succeed.

The importance of continuing to practice CBT techniques

The importance of continuing to practice CBT techniques cannot be overstated. CBT, or cognitive behavioral therapy, is a highly effective approach to treating a wide range of mental health conditions, including anxiety, depression, and PTSD. However, like any skill, it requires regular practice and refinement in order to be truly effective.

One of the key benefits of CBT is that it empowers individuals to take an active role in their own mental health. By teaching them to identify and challenge negative thought patterns and behaviors, CBT helps individuals develop the skills and tools they need to manage their symptoms and improve their overall quality of life. However, in order to reap the full benefits of CBT, it is important to continue practicing the techniques learned in therapy on a regular basis.

One of the simplest and most effective ways to continue practicing CBT techniques is through self-help books and resources. These materials can provide a wealth of information and guidance on how to apply CBT principles in daily life, and can help individuals stay motivated and engaged in their own mental health care. Additionally, many therapists offer CBT-based self-help materials as part of their treatment plans, which can be a valuable resource for individuals seeking to continue their therapy outside of the clinic.

Another important aspect of continuing to practice CBT techniques is seeking out ongoing support and feedback. This can be accomplished through ongoing therapy sessions, support groups, or other forms of peer-to-peer support. By connecting with others who are also working to improve their mental health, individuals can gain valuable insights and feedback on their progress, as well as find the motivation and support they need to stay on track.

In conclusion, the importance of continuing to practice CBT techniques cannot be overstated. By investing the time and effort needed to develop and refine these skills, individuals can take an active role in their own mental health care, and achieve lasting improvements in their overall well-being. Whether through self-help materials, ongoing therapy, or peer-to-peer support, there are many resources available to help individuals continue to build on the skills and techniques learned in CBT therapy.

Additional resources for further learning and growth.

Additional Resources for Further Learning and Growth

Congratulations on completing the comprehensive CBT course in a single book! By now, you should have a firm grasp of the fundamental principles and techniques of cognitive-behavioral therapy. However, there is always more to learn and explore in the field of CBT, especially as new research and innovations emerge.

If you're interested in furthering your knowledge and skills in CBT, here are some additional resources to consider:

1. Online Courses and Workshops

There are many online courses and workshops available that focus on specific areas of CBT, such as anxiety, depression, addiction, trauma, and more. These courses are often led by experienced CBT practitioners and offer interactive activities, case studies, and feedback to help you apply what you've learned.

2. Books and Journals

There are countless books and journals dedicated to CBT, ranging from introductory guides to advanced research and techniques. Some popular authors in the field include Aaron Beck, Judith Beck, David Burns, and Albert Ellis. Reading these materials can provide valuable insights and perspectives on CBT, as well as practical tips for working with clients.

3. Professional Organizations

Joining a professional organization can connect you with other CBT practitioners, provide access to training and resources, and offer opportunities for continuing education and certification. Some well-known CBT organizations include the Academy of Cognitive Therapy, the Beck Institute for Cognitive Behavior Therapy, and the Association for Behavioral and Cognitive Therapies.

4. Peer Support and Supervision

Connecting with other CBT practitioners and seeking supervision can be an invaluable source of support and growth. Peer support groups, online forums, and supervision sessions can offer feedback, guidance, and a space to reflect on your practice.

Remember, learning and growth are ongoing processes, and there is always more to discover and explore in the field of CBT. By utilizing these additional resources, you can continue to enhance your knowledge and skills, and ultimately, provide the best possible care for your clients.